There is No Race in the Heavenly Place

There is No Race in the Heavenly Place

THE RESURRECTED JESUS COULD ONLY BE
RECOGNIZED BY HIS WOUNDS AND THE
THINGS THAT HE DID.
HE WAS OMNI-RACIAL.

Don Morgan

For you are all children of God through faith in Christ Jesus. . . .There is no longer Jew or Gentile, slave or free, male and female. For you are all one in Christ Jesus.
Galatians 3:26, 28 NLT

But God, who is rich in mercy . . . made us alive together with Christ . . . and raised us up together, and made us sit together in the heavenly places in Christ Jesus.
Ephesians 2:4–6

To my Mennonite friends in Lancaster, Pennsylvania.

Your Light still shines in the world (Matthew 5:16).

Contents

Preface

*You saw me before I was born. Every day of my life was
recorded in your book. Every moment was laid out before
a single day had passed.*
Psalm 139:16 NLT

GOD SEES YOUR ENTIRE *life right now* from the perspective
of eternity. His omniscient, eternal nature allows Him to see all
things that ever have happened or ever will happen—*now*. He
sees you being born *now*. He sees what you did last year *now*. He
sees what you did ten years ago *now*. He sees what you did last
week *now*. He sees what you did yesterday *now*. He sees what
you are doing today. He sees you going to bed tonight. He sees
you waking up in the morning. He sees you going to work tomor-
row. He sees where you will be and what you will be doing fifty
years from now. He sees you on your death bed. He sees you
taking your last breath on earth.

There is nothing hidden from the eyes of the Almighty God.
Scripture tells us He saw Jeremiah the prophet *before* he was
born:

> *Then the word of the LORD came to me, saying:*
> *"Before I formed you in the womb I knew you; be-*
> *fore you were born I sanctified you; I ordained*
> *you a prophet to the nations." (Jeremiah 1:4–5)*

God knew Jeremiah the Jew before his father, Hilkiah, met and married his mother. He knew him before He clothed him in flesh. The Lord knew Jeremiah before any Jewish blood flowed through his veins. He knew him before He gave him a *temporary* flesh and blood racial identity. If you believe the New Testament of our Savior Jesus Christ, then you know that Jeremiah no longer has an identity based on flesh and blood. Paul the apostle, in his letter to the Corinthian church, made this fact very clear:

> *Now this I say, brethren, that flesh and blood cannot inherit the kingdom of God; nor does corruption inherit incorruption.* (1 Corinthians 15:50)

The New Living Translation version of this verse makes it even more understandable:

> *What I am saying, dear brothers and sisters, is that our physical bodies cannot inherit the Kingdom of God. These dying bodies cannot inherit what will last forever.* (1 Corinthians 15:50 NLT)

Many remarkable things happened in the life of Jeremiah the prophet. God called him into His prophetic ministry at a young age:

> *Then the word of the Lord came unto me, saying, before I formed thee in the belly I knew thee; and before thou camest forth out of the womb I sanctified thee, and I ordained thee a prophet unto the nations. Then said I, Ah, Lord God! behold, I cannot speak: for I am a child. But the Lord said unto me, Say not, I am a child: for thou shalt go to all that I shall send thee, and whatsoever I command thee thou shalt speak. . . . And the Lord said unto me, Behold, I have put*

my words in thy mouth. See, I have this day set thee over the nations and over the kingdoms, to root out, and to pull down, and to destroy, and to throw down, to build, and to plant. (Jeremiah 1:4–5, 9–10 KJV)

Many of these words spoken to Jeremiah are a *prophecy* of Jesus of Nazareth. God also gave Jesus words to speak (see John 14:10). And Jesus will one day return to earth and tear down the kingdoms of the world.

Jesus said He was with God His Father in Glory before the world was created:

"And now, O Father, glorify me together with yourself, with the glory which I had with you before the world was." (John 17:5)

God formed Jesus in the womb of the Virgin Mary:

And the angel said unto her, Fear not, Mary: for thou hast found favour with God. And, behold, thou shalt conceive in thy womb, and bring forth a son, and shalt call his name Jesus. (Luke 1:30–31 KJV)

Like Jeremiah, God called Jesus at a young age (see Luke 2:40–52). And also like Jeremiah, Jesus was a Prophet:

And when He had come into Jerusalem, all the city was moved, saying, "Who is this?" So the multitudes said, "This is Jesus, the prophet from Nazareth of Galilee." (Matthew 21:10–11)

It is likely that Jeremiah rose from the grave with the other Old Testament saints after the resurrection of Jesus:

And tombs opened. The bodies of many godly men and women who had died were raised from the dead. They left the cemetery after Jesus' resurrection, went into the holy city of Jerusalem, and appeared to many people. (Matthew 27:52–53 NLT)

Today, Jeremiah and these resurrected saints are seated in a heavenly place with the risen Christ. They have *fulfilled* Ephesians 2:4–7:

But God, who is rich in mercy, because of His great love with which He loved us, even when we were dead in trespasses, made us alive together with Christ (by grace you have been saved), and raised us up together, and made us sit together in the heavenly places in Christ Jesus, that in the ages to come He might show the exceeding riches of His grace in His kindness toward us in Christ Jesus.

The resurrected saints have also *fulfilled* Philippians 3:21 (NLT):

He will take our weak mortal bodies and change them into glorious bodies like his own, using the same power with which he will bring everything under his control.

All of us who love the Lord Jesus will one day live in the heavenly reality of Galatians 3:26–28 (NLT):

For you are all children of God through faith in Christ Jesus. And all who have been united with Christ in baptism have put on the character of Christ, like putting on new clothes. There

*is no longer Jew or Gentile, slave or free, male
and female. For you are all one in Christ Jesus.*

This Scripture passage from Paul's letter to the Galatian
church is *God's reality*. It expresses His eternal vision. It explains
how God sees you and me, Jeremiah the prophet, and the Old
Testament saints. God looked upon you through the *reality lens*
of Galatians 3:26–28 *before* you were born. He looked upon you
through this *reality* yesterday. He looks upon you through this
reality today. And He will view you *forever* through this reality
lens.

Your life on earth, with its passing temptations of the flesh
and its transitory fleshly racial identity, is a series of *temporary*
earthly grade school lessons. When you become a spiritual adult,
the temporary lesson of race will pass away.

*When I was a child, I spake as a child, I understood as a
child, I thought as a child: but when I became a man, I
put away childish things.* (1Corinthians 13:11 KJV)

What is the temporary lesson of race? The Founding Fathers
of our country had a glimpse of it—when they included this passage in the Declaration of Independence:

*We hold these truths to be self-evident, that all men
are created equal, that they are endowed by their
Creator with certain unalienable Rights that among
these are Life, Liberty and the pursuit of Happiness.*

The Founding Fathers were saying that God created human
beings with an innate freedom to determine and pursue his or
her own course in life.

The temporary lesson of race is our *spiritual challenge* from
God to become a spiritual adult—by living this passage from the

heart. Live and let live. Let everyone be free to choose his or her own course in life. Don't hang your expectations or your prejudicial attitudes on people that you don't know. Put into practice this wisdom from the Fathers—from your inner being. Apply it from your heart to all people, regardless of the color of their skin.

> *Owe no one anything except to love one another,*
> *for he who loves another has fulfilled the law. . . .*
> *Love does no harm to a neighbor; therefore love*
> *is the fulfillment of the law.* (Romans 13:8, 10)

Spiritual adults love the Lord their God with all their hearts. They have learned that their love for God will guide them. They realize that their love for God protects them. And they understand that their love for God causes them to prosper.

> *Seek the Kingdom of God above all else,*
> *and live righteously, and he will give you ev-*
> *erything you need.* (Matthew 6:33 NLT)

Spiritual adults find that their love for God also gives them spiritual wisdom, knowledge, and insight. They grasp the Bible's use of the word *predestinate*. They know that predestination is another way of saying that God sees all things *now* from His eternal perspective:

> *And we know that all things work together for good*
> *to them that love God, to them who are the called*
> *according to his purpose. For whom he did fore-*
> *know, he also did predestinate to be conformed to*
> *the image of his Son, that he might be the first-*
> *born among many brethren. Moreover whom he*
> *did predestinate, them he also called: and whom he*

called, them he also justified: and whom he justified,
them he also glorified. (Romans 8:28–30 KJV)

Spiritual adults *know* in their hearts that they are already in a glorified heavenly place with Jesus. They do their best to live their lives on earth in obedience to Colossians 3:1–3 (NLT):

> *Since you have been raised to new life with*
> *Christ, set your sights on the realities of heaven,*
> *where Christ sits in the place of honor at God's*
> *right hand. Think about the things of heaven,*
> *not the things of earth. For you died to this life,*
> *and your real life is hidden with Christ in God.*

Spiritual adults know in their hearts that there is no race in the heavenly place with Jesus. This knowledge is a *heartfelt reality* in them. Their own racial identity and the racial identity of others is about as important to them as the brand of toothpaste that they buy. They are unaffected by the racial rants of extremists or the apartheid words preached by some people in power. The Spirit that God has placed in them—from His heavenly high place—has caused them to be born again. They have been reborn from above. They are God's new creation.

> *Therefore, if anyone is in Christ, he is a new creation; old things have passed away; behold, all things have become new.* (2 Corinthians 5:17)

Then the Jews answered and said to Him, "Do we not
say rightly that you are a Samaritan and have a demon?"
John 8:48

CHAPTER 1

※

The N-Word of the New Testament

THE NATION OF ISRAEL was divided into two antagonistic kingdoms after the death of Solomon, King David's son. Rehoboam, the son of Solomon, ruled as king over the Southern kingdom of Judah. Jeroboam, the son of Nebat, became the first king of the breakaway Northern kingdom of Israel. One of the first things Jeroboam did was establish a religion based on calf worship—in order to satisfy the religious instincts of the people under his rule:

> Jeroboam thought to himself, "Unless I am careful, the kingdom will return to the dynasty of David. When these people go to Jerusalem to offer sacrifices at the Temple of the LORD, they will again give their allegiance to King Rehoboam of Judah. They will kill me and make him their king instead." So on the advice of his counselors, the king made two gold calves. He said to the people, "It is too much trouble for you

> to worship in Jerusalem. Look, Israel, these are the
> gods who brought you out of Egypt!" He placed these
> calf idols in Bethel and in Dan—at either end of his
> kingdom. But this became a great sin, for the people
> worshiped the idols, traveling as far north as Dan
> to worship the one there. (1 Kings 12:26–30 NLT)

The religious apostasy of the Northern kingdom of Israel
continued for many years. The fifth king to rule over the North
was King Omri. It was Omri who built the city of Samaria and
established it as the capital of the country. Omri was an evil king.
His desertion of the Lord God of the beloved King David was
worse than any king before him:

> But Omri did what was evil in the LORD's sight, even
> more than any of the kings before him. He followed
> the example of Jeroboam son of Nebat in all the sins
> he had committed and led Israel to commit. The peo-
> ple provoked the anger of the LORD, the God of Israel,
> with their worthless idols. (1 Kings 16:25–26 NLT)

After the death of Omri, his son Ahab reigned. Under King
Ahab and Queen Jezebel, the religious degeneration of Northern
Israel went from bad to worse. Ahab and Jezebel made Samaria
the seat of the worship of the false god Baal and the goddess
Asherah. The worship of Asherah—Jezebel's goddess—included
phallic symbols (Asherah poles), sex rites, and shrine prosti-
tutes. It is interesting that 800 years after Jezebel's death, the
resurrected Jesus complains about her presence in His church
(see Revelation 2:20–21).

Samaria was the headquarters of heathen worship in Israel.
They worshipped golden calves, the stars and the planets, and
Baal; they made sex worship shrines; they practiced witchcraft;

and they sacrificed their newborn children to pagan gods by burning them on fire altars:

> *They rejected all the commands of the LORD their God and made two calves from metal. They set up an Asherah pole and worshiped Baal and all the forces of heaven. They even sacrificed their own sons and daughters in the fire. They consulted fortune-tellers and practiced sorcery and sold themselves to evil, arousing the LORD's anger. Because the LORD was very angry with Israel, he swept them away from his presence. Only the tribe of Judah remained in the land.* (2 Kings 17:16–18 NLT)

God was angry with the Samaritans and caused them to be conquered by the Assyrian King Sargon II. Sargon deported the Samaritans to Assyria, and filled Samaria with people from various foreign countries:

> *For the children of Israel walked in all the sins of Jeroboam which he did; they did not depart from them, until the LORD removed Israel out of His sight, as He had said by all His servants the prophets. So Israel was carried away from their own land to Assyria, as it is to this day. Then the king of Assyria brought people from Babylon, Cuthah, Ava, Hamath, and from Sepharvaim, and placed them in the cities of Samaria instead of the children of Israel; and they took possession of Samaria and dwelt in its cities.* (2 Kings 17:22–24)

These foreign colonists had a problem with wild lions in the land of Samaria. For this reason, the Assyrian king decided to have them taught how to worship the God of Israel. The king returned one of the deported priests to Samaria, and the priest instructed the people in the proper way to worship Israel's God. So, in addition to the many gods the foreign settlers worshipped in Samaria, they also worshipped the God of Israel:

> The king of Assyria then commanded, "Send one of the exiled priests back to Samaria. Let him live there and teach the new residents the religious customs of the God of the land." So one of the priests who had been exiled from Samaria returned to Bethel and taught the new residents how to worship the LORD. But these various groups of foreigners also continued to worship their own gods. In town after town where they lived, they placed their idols at the pagan shrines that the people of Samaria had built. Those from Babylon worshiped idols of their god Succoth-benoth. Those from Cuthah worshiped their god Nergal. And those from Hamath worshiped Ashima. The Avvites worshiped their gods Nibhaz and Tartak. And the people from Sepharvaim even burned their own children as sacrifices to their gods Adrammelech and Anammelech. These new residents worshiped the LORD, but they also appointed from among themselves all sorts of people as priests to offer sacrifices at their places of worship. And though they worshiped the LORD, they continued to follow their own gods according to the religious customs of the nations from which they came. And this is still going on today. They continue to follow their former practices instead of truly worshiping the LORD and obeying the decrees, regulations, instructions, and commands he gave the descendants of Jacob, whose name he changed to Israel. (2 Kings 17:27–34 NLT)

Over time, the religious authorities and the priests in Jerusalem grew to hate the Samaritans. Seven hundred and fifty years after Samaria was conquered and repopulated with foreigners, the word *Samaritan* had become the N-word of that time. The ruling priests and religious leaders called Jesus a Samaritan:

> *Then the Jews answered and said to Him, "Do we not say rightly that you are a Samaritan and have a demon?"* (John 8:48)

Take a look at Jesus's answer to the Samaritan denigration:

> *Jesus answered, "I do not have a demon; but I honor My Father, and you dishonor me."* (John 8:49)

Jesus ignored and disregarded the racist slur. He did this because He *knew* He had the Spirit of God in His heart. He knew where He came from and where He was going. And he knew that Psalm 139:13–14 was written about Him:

> *For You* [Father God] *formed my inward parts; you covered me in my mother's womb. I will praise you, for I am fearfully and wonderfully made; marvelous are your works, and that my soul knows very well.*

Jesus lived with God's heavenly place in His heart. His essence was filled with the reality of heaven. *His heart had no room to receive the devil-inspired hate the Synagogue leaders tried to serve Him.* When they slapped Him with the N-word slur, He mentally turned the other cheek.

> *But I say unto you, that ye resist not evil: but whosoever shall smite thee on thy right cheek, turn to him the other also.* (Matthew 5:39 KJV)

Jesus said that if you are his disciple, the world will treat you just like it treated Him:

> *"If the world hates you, you know that it hated Me before it hated you. If you were of the world, the world would love its own. Yet because you are not of the world, but I chose you out of the world, therefore the world hates you."* (John 15:18–19)

If you are a person of color who belongs to Jesus and find that some people dislike you because of your race, you have five reasons to rejoice and make yourself glad:

1. Jesus also was despised and rejected:

> *He is despised and rejected of men; a man of sorrows, and acquainted with grief: and we hid as it were our faces from him; he was despised, and we esteemed him not.* (Isaiah 53:3 KJV)

2. Jesus was hated for no good reason:

> *"But as it is, they have seen everything I did, yet they still hate me and my Father. This fulfills what is written in their Scriptures: 'They hated me without cause.' "* (John 15:24–25 NLT)

3. You have been called to follow in the footsteps of the suffering of Christ:

> *For God is pleased with you when, conscious of his will, you patiently endure unfair treatment. . . . For God called you to do good, even if it means suffering, just as Christ suffered for you. He is your example, and you must follow in his steps.* (1 Peter 2:19, 21 NLT)

4. God has given you the opportunity to carry the cross of Jesus's suffering every day that you face bigotry:

> *Then He said to them all, "If anyone desires to come after Me, let him deny himself, and take up his cross daily, and follow Me."* (Luke 9:23)

5. Jesus said you are blessed along with God's prophets:

> *Blessed are you when men hate you, and when they exclude you, and revile you, and cast out your name as evil, for the Son of Man's sake. Rejoice in that day and leap for joy! For indeed your reward is great in heaven, for in like manner their fathers did to the prophets.* (Luke 6:22–23)

Perhaps today you feel like you are on the outside of society looking in. But if you keep your faith in God, even though you walk through the valley of the shadow of hate, even though you walk through the reality of Matthew 10:22, you will one day be inside the gates of God's house. At that blessed time, it is likely that someone that the world considers beautiful and blessed today will be on the *outside* of the kingdom of God looking *in* at you. *Someone* is going to fulfil Matthew 8:11–12:

> *"And I say to you that many will come from east and west, and sit down with Abraham, Isaac, and Jacob in the kingdom of heaven. But the sons of the kingdom will be cast out into outer darkness. There will be weeping and gnashing of teeth."*

Perhaps you think the answer to the racial discord in the nation today lies in political activism. Perhaps you feel the need to fight for your rights. People in our country have been fighting for what they perceive are their racial rights since before the Civil War. Abraham Lincoln was shot dead on the altar of racial disharmony. Martin Luther King Jr., perhaps the greatest political activist since Gandhi, was shot dead on the altar of racial disharmony. People are still being murdered today on the altar of racial disharmony. Yet the racial discord continues. The answer is *not* in political activism. No amount of political activism on earth can stop the end-time prophecy of racial strife that Jesus pronounced:

> *"For nation will rise against nation, and kingdom against kingdom. And there will be famines, pestilences, and earthquakes in various places. All these are the beginning of sorrows."* (Matthew 24:7–8)

The word *nation* in this passage means "race" in the original Greek translation. In other words:

> *For race will rise against race, and kingdom against kingdom . . .*

Jesus is not a Republican. Jesus is not a Democrat, He's not an Independent. He's not a political activist. He is God. And He has said that His followers do *not* fight for political purposes in this present age:

> *Jesus answered, "My Kingdom is not an earthly kingdom. If it were, my followers would fight to keep me from being handed over to the Jewish leaders. But my Kingdom is not of this world."* (John 18:36 NLT)

There *is* a lot of fighting that you need to do. But it's a *spiritual fight.* You need to fight against temptation and sin. You need to fight to discern right from wrong. You need to fight to always choose the right. You need to fight to *love your enemies*. And you need to fight to learn how to *turn the other cheek*.

> *For we are not fighting against flesh-and-blood enemies, but against evil rulers and authorities of the unseen world, against mighty powers in this dark world, and against evil spirits in the heavenly places.* (Ephesians 6:12 NLT)

The Word of God says the devil will dominate the affairs of men and women in the natural world until he is destroyed in the Lake of Fire. He will continue to stir up racial strife in the world until Revelation 20:10 happens:

> *The devil, who deceived them, was cast into the lake of fire and brimstone where the beast and the false prophet are. And they will be tormented day and night forever and ever.* (Revelation 20:10)

Until the day that the devil becomes toast, he will exercise the worldly power that he stole from Adam and Eve in the Garden of Eden.

> *Then the devil, taking Him up on a high mountain, showed Him all the kingdoms of the world in a moment of time. And the devil said to Him, "All this authority I will give You, and their glory; for this has been delivered to me, and I give it to whomever I wish. Therefore, if You will worship before me, all will be Yours."* (Luke 4:5–7)

Paul the apostle called the devil a commander:

You used to live in sin, just like the rest of the world, obeying the devil—the commander of the powers in the unseen world. (Ephesians 2:2 NLT)

Jesus called the devil the ruler ("prince" in the KJV translation) of the world:

"I don't have much more time to talk to you, because the ruler of this world approaches. He has no power over me." (John 14:30 NLT)

Jesus said we are to be in the world but not *of* the world. He prayed to His Father that we would be protected from "the evil one."

"I have given them your word; and the world has hated them because they are not of the world, just as I am not of the world. I do not pray that you should take them out of the world, but that you should keep them from the evil one. They are not of the world, just as I am not of the world." (John 17:14–16)

Is it possible that all the fighting that people do in the world in the name of politics is nothing more than "big devils fighting bigger devils" and Satan-inspired people fighting to dominate each other?

While we live in this world of different shapes and colors of men and women, our spiritual challenge is to become a spiritual adult and express the heavenly wisdom of James 3:17–18 (NLT):

But the wisdom from above is first of all pure. It is also peace loving, gentle at all times, and willing to yield to others. It is full of mercy and good deeds. It shows no favoritism and is always sincere. And those who are peacemakers will plant seeds of peace and reap a harvest of righteousness.

After Jesus rose from the dead early on Sunday morning, the first person who saw him was Mary Magdalene, the woman from whom he had cast out seven demons. She went to the disciples, who were grieving and weeping, and told them what had happened. But when she told them that Jesus was alive and she had seen him, they didn't believe her. Afterward he appeared in a different form to two of his followers who were walking from Jerusalem into the country.
Mark 16:9–12 NLT

CHAPTER 2

The Foreigner on the Road to Emmaus

ON THE THIRD DAY after Jesus was crucified, Cleopas and his wife were returning to their home in the village of Emmaus. They had followed Jesus of Nazareth, believing He was the Messiah from God who would save the nation of Israel from Roman oppression. Their hopes were shattered when they saw Jesus accused of treason by a vote of their religious leaders, and executed by the Roman government. They saw Him hanging naked on a cross. They saw the brutal soldiers gambling for His coat. They saw Him breathe His last breath. And they saw Him hastily buried in a nearby tomb. His disciples and many of the residents of Jerusalem saw the same things unfold. It was the talk of the town. But three days later, the once crazy Mary Magdalene was running around telling everyone that she saw Him alive in the cemetery garden. She said He looked like a different man, that she'd mistaken Him for the garden caretaker. She didn't know who He was until He called her name. Then she said she *knew* it was the Teacher:

> *She* [Mary Magdalene] *turned to leave and saw someone standing there. It was Jesus, but she didn't recognize him. "Dear woman, why are you crying?" Jesus asked her. "Who are you looking for?" She thought he was the gardener. "Sir," she said, "if you have taken him away, tell me where you have put him, and I will go and get him." "Mary!" Jesus said. She turned to him and cried out, "Rabboni!" (which is Hebrew for "Teacher").* (John 20:14–16 NLT)

Cleopas and his wife were intensely discussing their disappointment following the death of Jesus. They were also talking about the unbelieveable report of Mary Magdalene. During the conversation, one of the travelers on the road caught up to them and walked beside them while they talked. Then the Man asked them a question about their conversation:

> *So it was, while they conversed and reasoned, that Jesus Himself drew near and went with them. But their eyes were restrained, so that they did not know Him. And He said to them, "What kind of conversation is this that you have with one another as you walk and are sad?" Then the one whose name was Cleopas answered and said to Him, "Are you the only stranger in Jerusalem, and have you not known the things which happened there in these days?" And He said to them, "What things?" So they said to Him, "The things concerning Jesus of Nazareth, who was a Prophet mighty in deed and word before God and all the people, and how the chief priests and our rulers delivered Him to be condemned to death, and crucified Him. But we were hoping that it was He who was going to redeem Israel.* (Luke 24:15–21)

This stranger on the road to Emmaus was Jesus. The word *stranger* in the Greek language means "foreigner." To Cleopas and his wife, the now-resurrected Jesus looked like a foreigner. Cleopas, in effect, is saying to Him, "You must be the only foreigner in town who hasn't heard the news about Jesus of Nazareth."

While they were walking along, the Teacher began to teach. He taught them all the predictions about the Messiah in the writings of the Old Testament prophets:

> *And beginning at Moses and all the Prophets, He expounded to them in all the Scriptures the things concerning Himself.* (Luke 24:27)

A spiritual fire began to burn in the hearts of Cleopas and his wife. They invited Him into their home to spend the night. But an amazing thing happened when they sat down for their evening meal. The stranger took the bread, broke it, and prayed just like Jesus of Nazareth! Then *something happened* to the eyes of the man and his wife, and they could *see* that He was Jesus:

> *Now it came to pass, as He sat at the table with them, that He took bread, blessed and broke it, and gave it to them. Then their eyes were opened and they knew Him; and He vanished from their sight. And they said to one another, "Did not our heart burn within us while He talked with us on the road, and while He opened the Scriptures to us?" So they rose up that very hour and returned to Jerusalem, and found the eleven and those who were with them gathered together, saying, "The Lord is risen indeed, and has appeared to Simon!" And they told about the things that had happened on the road, and how He was known to them in the breaking of bread.* (Luke 24:30–35)

Cleopas and his wife were not the only ones to recognize the resurrected Jesus by His *actions* rather than by the appearance of His face. Peter, recognized Him as the Messiah when Jesus performed the miracle of the huge fish catch and called him to preach (see Luke 5:3–10). After His resurrection, Peter and six other disciples decided to try their luck at fishing again. As before, they fished all night and didn't catch anything. In the morning, a stranger stood on the shore. He called to them and asked them if they caught any fish. When they said no, He told them that they would catch fish if they threw the net on the right side of the boat. They threw the net and—boom—another miraculous fish catch! When they caught up with the stranger on the shore, they didn't *dare* ask Him who He was. They *knew* who He was. They knew He was Jesus by His miracle, *not* by the appearance of His face:

> *Simon Peter went up and dragged the net to land, full of large fish, one hundred and fifty-three; and although there were so many, the net was not broken. Jesus said to them, "Come and eat breakfast." Yet none of the disciples dared ask Him, "Who are you?"—knowing that it was the Lord.* (John 21:11–12)

The disciple known as "doubting Thomas" heard the rumor that the resurrected Jesus didn't look the same, but he didn't believe it. He thought it must be an imposter:

> *Now Thomas, called the Twin, one of the twelve, was not with them when Jesus came. The other disciples therefore said to him, "We have seen the Lord." So he said to them, "Unless I see in His hands the print of the nails, and put my finger into the print of the nails, and put my hand into His side, I*

*will not believe." And after eight days His disciples
were again inside, and Thomas with them. Jesus
came, the doors being shut, and stood in the midst,
and said, "Peace to you!" Then He said to Thomas,
"Reach your finger here, and look at my hands; and
reach your hand here, and put it into my side. Do
not be unbelieving, but believing." (John 20:24–27)*

Thomas the unbeliever became a believer when he saw the
wounds in the hands and the side of the stranger.

But not everyone believed that Jesus rose from the grave.
The changed appearance of His face was too big of an obstacle
for some of His followers. On the day Jesus rose into heaven,
there were doubters in the crowd of disciples who watched Him
ascend:

*Then the eleven disciples went away into Galilee,
to the mountain which Jesus had appointed for
them. When they saw Him, they worshiped
Him; but some doubted. (Matthew 28:16–17)*

Why did Jesus so radically change the appearance of His face
when He rose from the grave? What is the lesson here?

After rising from the dead, Jesus the Jew was no longer a Jew.
He had become omni-racial. He is my God and your God.

Our God doesn't look upon the outward appearance of people. He looks upon the heart:

*But the LORD said to Samuel, "Don't judge by his
appearance or height, for I have rejected him. The
LORD doesn't see things the way you see them. People
judge by outward appearance, but the LORD looks at
the heart." (1 Samuel 16:7 NLT, emphasis added)*

God doesn't even notice your black skin or your white skin. He sees only the attitude of your heart.

Then he [Jesus] said, "When I was with you before, I told you that everything written about me in the Law of Moses and the prophets and in the Psalms must be fulfilled." Luke 24:44 NLT

CHAPTER 3

The Prophecy of Moses and His Ethiopian Wife

Then Miriam and Aaron spoke against Moses because of the Ethiopian woman whom he had married; for he had married an Ethiopian woman. So they said, "Has the LORD indeed spoken only through Moses? Has He not spoken through us also?" And the LORD heard it. . . . Suddenly the LORD said to Moses, Aaron, and Miriam, "Come out, you three, to the tabernacle of meeting!" So the three came out. Then the LORD came down in the pillar of cloud and stood in the door of the tabernacle, and called Aaron and Miriam. And they both went forward. Then He said, "Hear now My words: "If there is a prophet among you, I, the LORD, make Myself known to him in a vision; I speak to him in a dream. Not so with my servant Moses; He is faithful in all my house. I speak with him face to face, even plainly, and not in dark sayings; and he sees the form of the LORD. Why then were you not afraid to speak against my servant Moses?" So the anger of the LORD was aroused against them, and He departed. And when the cloud departed from above the tabernacle, suddenly Miriam became leprous, as white as snow. *Then Aaron turned toward Miriam, and there she was, a leper.* Numbers 12:1–10

THE LIFE OF MOSES was a prophetic foretelling of the life of Jesus. Moses was the most powerful prophet in the Old Testament:

> *There has never been another prophet in Israel like Moses, whom the LORD knew face to face. The LORD sent him to perform all the miraculous signs and wonders in the land of Egypt against Pharaoh, and all his servants, and his entire land. With mighty power, Moses performed terrifying acts in the sight of all Israel.* (Deuteronomy 34:10–12 NLT)

Jesus was the most powerful prophet in the New Testament:

> *"Jesus of Nazareth . . . was a Prophet mighty in deed and word before God and all the people."* (Luke 24:19)

An evil king tried to kill Moses when he was an infant:

> *Then Pharaoh gave this order to all his people: "Throw every newborn Hebrew boy into the Nile River. But you may let the girls live."* (Exodus 1:22 NLT)

An evil king also tried to kill Jesus when He was a child:

> *Now when they had departed, behold, an angel of the Lord appeared to Joseph in a dream, saying, "Arise,*

> *take the young Child and His mother, flee to Egypt, and*
> *stay there until I bring you word; for Herod will seek*
> *the young Child to destroy Him."* (Matthew 2:13)

Moses married an Ethiopian woman named Zipporah. She was the daughter of Jethro, the priest of Midian (see Exodus 2:16–21, Exodus 3:1).

Jesus likened the kingdom of God to a King preparing a wedding for his Son:

> *"The kingdom of heaven is like a certain king who*
> *arranged a marriage for his son, and sent out his ser-*
> *vants to call those who were invited to the wedding; and*
> *they were not willing to come."* (Matthew 22:2–3)

The King in this parable is God. The Son is Jesus the Bridegroom (see Matthew 9:14–15). The people who refused to come to the wedding are the Jews who rejected and crucified Jesus. These Jews are the *spiritual* bride who refused to marry the Son. God then chose another (non-Jewish) bride for His Son—the Gentile Church. Take a look at what the apostle Paul said to the Corinthian (Gentile) church:

> *For I am jealous for you with the jealousy of God*
> *himself. I promised you as a pure bride to one*
> *husband—Christ.* (2 Corinthians 11:2 NLT)

Also take a look at what Paul said to the Jews in Rome when they would not fully accept his preaching about Jesus:

> *"So I want you to know that this salvation*
> *from God has also been offered to the Gentiles,*
> *and they will accept it."* (Acts 28:28 NLT)

Jesus was a prophet who "married" a Gentile bride—the Church.

Moses was a prophet who married a Gentile bride—an Ethiopian woman.

Moses made intercessory pleadings to God for the sins of his people when he was in God's presence on the holy mountain of Sinai:

> *Then Moses pleaded with the LORD his God, and said: "LORD, why does your wrath burn hot against your people whom you have brought out of the land of Egypt with great power and with a mighty hand? Why should the Egyptians speak, and say, 'He brought them out to harm them, to kill them in the mountains, and to consume them from the face of the earth'? Turn from your fierce wrath, and relent from this harm to your people. Remember Abraham, Isaac, and Israel, your servants, to whom you swore by your own self, and said to them, 'I will multiply your descendants as the stars of heaven; and all this land that I have spoken of I give to your descendants, and they shall inherit it forever.' " So the Lord relented from the harm which He said He would do to His people. (Exodus 32:11–14)*

Jesus is in the high and holy mountain of heaven today. He is the High Priest who makes intercession to God on behalf of you and me:

> *Therefore He [Jesus] is also able to save to the uttermost those who come to God through Him, since He always lives to make intercession for them. For such a High Priest was fitting for us, who is holy, harmless,*

undefiled, separate from sinners, and has become higher than the heavens. (Hebrews 7:25–26)

While Moses was on Mount Sinai, God gave him instructions to build a sanctuary for worship:

"And let them make me a sanctuary, that I may dwell among them. According to all that I show you, that is, the pattern of the tabernacle and the pattern of all its furnishings, just so you shall make it." (Exodus 25:8–9)

Jesus said He was going to His Father's house in heaven to prepare a place for His followers:

"In My Father's house are many mansions; if it were not so, I would have told you. I go to prepare a place for you." (John 14:2)

Moses was on the Mount Sinai for a long time talking to God—forty days and forty nights. The people down below watching for Moses to return got bored waiting. The majority decided to make their own god, create a religion, and have a wild naked party (see Exodus 32:1–35). Moses returned from the mountain and found his people in an idolatrous, degenerate, sinful, and backslidden state. The people paid a terrible price for their depravity. Many of them died, and Moses went back up the mountain to pray to God for them.

Moses on Mount Sinai is a prophecy of Jesus in heaven. Jesus has been back in heaven for a long time now (about 2,000 years). Many people on earth have gotten bored with the message of Jesus Christ. Many churches have become mostly social clubs instead of places that extends the joy and peace of God to all. Luke-

warm church people and unchurched worldly people are fulfilling the prophecy of Isaiah by worshipping the god of technology:

> *Their land is also full of idols; they wor-*
> *ship the work of their own hands, that which*
> *their own fingers have made.* (Isaiah 2:8)

One day, Jesus is going to return from heaven. When He
comes back, the idolaters, the lukewarm, the unbelievers, and
the backsliders will pay a terrible price for their sins:

> *Then everyone—the kings of the earth, the rulers,*
> *the generals, the wealthy, the powerful, and every*
> *slave and free person—all hid themselves in the*
> *caves and among the rocks of the mountains. And*
> *they cried to the mountains and the rocks, "Fall on*
> *us and hide us from the face of the one who sits on*
> *the throne and from the wrath of the Lamb. For*
> *the great day of their wrath has come, and who*
> *is able to survive?"* (Revelation 6:15–17 NLT)

The preachers and the Bible teachers who refuse to teach
the story of racism and interracial marriage in Numbers 12 (the
story of Moses and his Ethiopian bride) will be among those
hiding in caves when Jesus returns. The Christian Evangelical
Movement—the Moral Majority—was born out of opposition to
interracial dating (in support of Bob Jones University). Many so-
called Evangelicals will be hiding in the hills—shaking in their
boots when Jesus returns, because they failed to become spiritual adults and teach their congregations that there is no race in
the heavenly place.

But when his [King Nebuchadnezzar's] *heart was lifted up, and his spirit was hardened in pride, he was deposed from his kingly throne, and they took his glory from him. Then he was driven from the sons of men, his heart was made like the beasts, and his dwelling was with the wild donkeys. They fed him with grass like oxen, and his body was wet with the dew of heaven, till he knew that the Most High God rules in the kingdom of men, and appoints over it whomever He chooses.*
Daniel 5:20–21

CHAPTER 4

The Proud King Who
Symbolized the Devil

*That very hour the word was fulfilled concerning
Nebuchadnezzar; he was driven from men and ate
grass like oxen; his body was wet with the dew of
heaven till his hair had grown like eagles' feath-
ers and his nails like birds' claws. Daniel 4:33*

NEBUCHADNEZZAR IS THE MOST well-known king of ancient Babylon. He reigned from 604 to 562 BC. He was a warrior-
king as well as a builder. He built the famous Hanging Gardens
of Babylon and the Babylonian Ishtar Gate—both Seven Wonders of the Ancient World. He also made Babylon a center of
power and influence through his conquests of Assyria, Syria,
Palestine, and Egypt. Nebuchadnezzar destroyed Jerusalem and
the Temple of the Lord when Zedekiah, king of Judah, rebelled
against him:

On August 14 of that year, which was the nineteenth year of King Nebuchadnezzar's reign, Nebuzaradan, the captain of the guard and an official of the Babylonian king, arrived in Jerusalem. He burned down the Temple of the Lord, the royal palace, and all the houses of Jerusalem. He destroyed all the important buildings in the city. Then he supervised the entire Babylonian army as they tore down the walls of Jerusalem on every side. Nebuzaradan, the captain of the guard, then took as exiles the rest of the people who remained in the city, the defectors who had declared their allegiance to the king of Babylon, and the rest of the population. (2 Kings 25:8–11 NLT)

Among the exiles that Nebuchadnezzar deported from Jerusalem were four boys named Daniel, Shadrach, Meshach, and Abednego. God blessed the four of them with the gifts of wisdom and knowledge. Daniel also had the prophetic ability to interpret visions and dreams:

God gave these four young men an unusual aptitude for understanding every aspect of literature and wisdom. And God gave Daniel the special ability to interpret the meanings of visions and dreams. (Daniel 1:17 NLT)

One night, king Nebuchadnezzar was troubled by a dream that he couldn't remember. He commanded his council of astrologers, soothsayers, wizards, and all the wise men in Babylon, to recall the dream for him and give him the interpretation. When they failed to recall and interpret his dream, he ordered that they all be executed (see Daniel 2:1–47). Daniel saved the magi and the wise men by interpreting the king's dream. Nebuchadnezzar then made Daniel the prime minister of Babylon and chief of the magi and the wise men. At Daniel's request, the king also made Daniel's three friends *political* rulers of the Babylonian provinces:

> The king said to Daniel, "Truly, your God is the greatest of gods, the Lord over kings, a revealer of mysteries, for you have been able to reveal this secret." Then the king appointed Daniel to a high position and gave him many valuable gifts. He made Daniel ruler over the whole province of Babylon, as well as chief over all his wise men. At Daniel's request, the king appointed Shadrach, Meshach, and Abednego to be in charge of all the affairs of the province of Babylon, while Daniel remained in the king's court. (Daniel 2:47–49 NLT)

Nebuchadnezzar, as king of Babylon, ruled most of the Middle East. He became extremely proud of himself because of his accomplishments:

> "As he looked out across the city, he said, 'Look at this great city of Babylon! By my own mighty power, I have built this beautiful city as my royal residence to display my majestic splendor.' " (Daniel 4:30 NLT)

God punished him for his pride by transforming him into a man-beast:

> "Let his [Nebuchadnezzar's] heart be changed from that of a man, Let him be given the heart of a beast, and let seven times pass over him." (Daniel 4:16)

Nebuchadnezzar the king-man-beast is a prophecy of the rise of the Man of Lawlessness (the Antichrist or Beast) at the end of the world:

> Then the man of lawlessness will be revealed . . . This man will come to do the work of Satan with counterfeit power and signs and miracles. He will use every kind of evil deception to fool those on their way to destruction. (2 Thessalonians 2:8–10 NLT)

In Revelation 12:9, Satan (the Dragon) is once and for all kicked out of heaven. Chapter thirteen describes a man who rises from the sea of humanity and becomes possessed by the outcast Dragon. This Satan-possessed man becomes the political leader of the entire world. His spiritual name is the Beast:

> And they worshipped the dragon which gave power unto the beast: and they worshipped the beast, saying, Who is like unto the beast? Who is able to make war with him? (Revelation 13:4 KJV)

The spiritual name of the fallen end-time world is Babylon:

> He gave a mighty shout: "Babylon is fallen—that great city is fallen! She has become a home for demons. She is a hideout for every foul spirit, a hideout for every foul vulture and every foul and dreadful animal. For all the nations have fallen because of the wine of her passionate immorality. The kings of the world have committed adultery with her. (Revelation 18:2–3 NLT)

The man whose spiritual name is the Beast becomes the great warrior-king of the end-time world. King Nebuchadnezzar, king of the original Babylon, is a prophecy of this man. The Dragon (devil) eventually causes all the world to worship him—and in doing so, the world inadvertently worships Satan.

> *All the world marveled and followed the beast. . . . It was granted to him to make war with the saints and to overcome them. And authority was given him over every tribe, tongue, and nation. All who dwell on the earth will worship him. . . . And he deceives those who dwell on the earth by those signs which he was granted to do in the sight of the beast, telling those who dwell on the earth to make an image to the beast . . . and cause as many as would not worship the image of the beast to be killed.* (Revelation 13:3, 7–8, 14–15)

The image of the Beast is a worldwide political system that everyone must adhere to. If not, they will be attacked and killed by the Dragon—also known as the Beast or the Antichrist.

There is a chapter in King Nebuchadnezzar's life that is a prophetic prequel to the end-time image of the Beast. In Daniel 3, Nebuchadnezzar sets up a ninety-foot tall golden idol. Then he invites all the politicians in the Babylonian world to dedicate themselves to this image. Daniel was not invited because he was a holy and religious man. *His absence is an omen of the time that the devil will outlaw the faith of Abraham, Isaac, Jacob, and Jesus.* This golden idol is intended to eventually replace religion as we know it today. It will be Satan's replacement for Christianly, Judaism, Islam, Buddhism, Hinduism, and every other religion in the world. *It will become the highest aspiration of mankind.* The golden idol that Nebuchadnezzar forced the politicians to accept is destined to become a worldwide secular religion and represents the aspirational idea of Democracy—the rule by the majority.

THERE IS NO RACE IN THE HEAVENLY PLACE

Majority rule is one of the best tools in the devil's toolbox. Using Democracy, the devil has legalized abortion, teenage sex, homosexuality, transvestites, drug use, risqué clothing, ungodly movies and games for children, Jim Crow laws, and other things that are abominations to our holy God.

The Antichrist, like Hitler, will rise to power through political means. This is how Hitler became the absolute dictator of Germany, ultimately influencing the entire world to go to war. Likewise, the Antichrist will use peaceful democratic processes to influence all the governments of the world until he becomes the President of the Nations. Then he will throw the entire world into the Fiery Furnace of World War III, marshaling the world's military forces against Israel (Zechariah 12:3–9). Israel will be attacked because she will refuse to submit to the quasi-religious idol of world Democracy.

When Shadrach, Meshach, and Abednego refused to bow down with the other politicians, Nebuchadnezzar showed his true colors:

> *"We want to make it clear to you, Your Majesty that we will never serve your gods or worship the gold statue you have set up."* Nebuchadnezzar was so furious with Shadrach, Meshach, and Abednego that his face became distorted with rage. He commanded that the furnace be heated seven times hotter than usual. Then he ordered some of the strongest men of his army to bind Shadrach, Meshach, and Abednego and throw them into the blazing furnace. So they tied them up and threw them into the furnace, fully dressed in their pants, turbans, robes, and other garments. (Daniel 3:18–21 NLT)

God rescued Shadrach, Meshach, and Abednego from the fiery furnace, but their harrowing ordeal foreshadows the day that the *real* King of kings will throw the false king of kings into the Lake of Fire:

> *I saw the beast, the kings of the earth, and their armies, gathered together to make war against Him [Jesus] who sat on the horse and against His army. Then the beast was captured, and with him the false prophet who worked signs in his presence . . . These two were cast alive into the lake of fire burning with brimstone.* (Revelation 19:19–20)

The prophet Daniel said God made Nebuchadnezzar a king of kings. He was the golden head of *earthly* kings:

> *You, O king, are a king of kings. For the God of heaven has given you a kingdom, power, strength, and glory; and wherever the children of men dwell, or the beasts of the field and the birds of the heaven, He has given them into your hand, and has made you ruler over them all—you are this head of gold.* (Daniel 2:37–38)

Nebuchadnezzar was a symbol of the devil—the fallen angelic being who rules over the kingdoms of this present world.

At the end-time, when Jesus returns to usher in the new world of the kingdom of God, His title will be King of all kings and Lord of all lords.

How art thou fallen from heaven, O Lucifer, son of the morning! How art thou cut down to the ground, which didst weaken the nations! For thou hast said in thine heart, I will ascend into heaven, I will exalt my throne above the stars of God: I will sit also upon the mount of the congregation, in the sides of the north: I will ascend above the heights of the clouds; I will be like the most High. Yet thou shalt be brought down to hell, to the sides of the pit. They that see thee shall narrowly look upon thee, and consider thee, saying, is this the man that made the earth to tremble, that did shake kingdoms; that made the world as a wilderness, and destroyed the cities thereof; that opened not the house of his prisoners?

Isaiah 14:12–17 KJV

CHAPTER 5

The Gorgeous Angel Who Started a Race War

Moreover the word of the LORD came to me, say-ing, "Son of man, take up a lamentation for the [Satan-possessed] king of Tyre, and say to him, 'Thus says the Lord GOD: "You were the seal of per-fection, full of wisdom and perfect in beauty. You were in Eden, the garden of God; every precious stone was your covering. . . . You were the anoint-ed cherub who covers; I established you; you were on the holy mountain of God; you walked back and forth in the midst of fiery stones." Ezekiel 28:11–14

THE PROPHET EZEKIEL'S PARABOLIC song about the alle-gorical king of Tyre is very revealing. The king was possessed by a beautiful, proud, wise, intelligent, and wicked evil spirit—the fallen angel Lucifer (whose name means "bright shining star"). He has several other names such as the devil, Satan, Beelzebub, the Dragon, and the Serpent. The bright and resplendent Lucifer possessed a serpent in the Garden of Eden. Beautiful Lucifer inspired the serpent to deceive Eve and has been deceiving and lying to mankind ever since.

Jesus said the devil is the father of lies:

> *"You are of your father the devil, and the desires of your father you want to do. He was a murderer from the beginning, and does not stand in the truth, because there is no truth in him. When he speaks a lie, he speaks from his own resources, for he is a liar and the father of it."* (John 8:44)

You can see from the words of Jesus that Lucifer is also the father of *murder*. Jesus is telling us that the devil inspired Cain to kill his brother Able.

How did someone so handsome become so wickedly evil? It started when Lucifer became narcissistically proud and obsessed by his own glamor:

> *"Your heart was filled with pride because of all your beauty. Your wisdom was corrupted by your love of splendor."* (Ezekiel 28:17 NLT)

Ezekiel, in another of his prophetic parables, reveals to us that Pharaoh—the king of Egypt—was also possessed by Lucifer's spirit of narcissistic pride. Ezekiel personifies Pharaoh as the tallest and most beautiful cedar tree in the Garden of Eden. All the other trees in Eden are jealous and envious of him. When this tall and beautiful tree is finally destroyed by God, it causes all the nations of the world to shake:

I made the nations to shake at the sound of his [Pharaoh's] *fall, when I cast him down to hell with them that descend into the pit: and all the trees of Eden, the choice and best of Lebanon . . . They also went down into hell with him unto them that be slain with the sword.* (Ezekiel 31:16–17 KJV)

"Son of man, say to Pharaoh king of Egypt and to his multitude: 'Whom are you like in your greatness? . . . The cedars in the garden of God could not hide it; the fir trees were not like its boughs, and the chestnut trees were not like its branches; no tree in the garden of God was like it in beauty. *I made it beautiful with a multitude of branches, So that all the trees of Eden envied it, that were in the garden of God.'* "Therefore thus says the Lord GOD: 'Because you have increased in height, and it set its top among the thick boughs, and its heart was lifted up in its height, therefore I will deliver it into the hand of the mighty one* [Jesus] *of the nations, and he shall surely deal with it; I have driven it out for its wickedness. . . . To which of the trees in Eden will you then be likened in glory and greatness? Yet you shall be brought down with the trees of Eden to the depths of the earth; you shall lie in the midst of the uncircumcised, with those slain by the sword. This is Pharaoh and all his multitude,' says the Lord GOD."* (Ezekiel 31:2, 8–11, 18)

The tall, beautiful Pharaoh-tree that was in the Garden of God represents Lucifer. *The envious trees of Eden represent the fallen angels that were mesmerized by Satan's attractiveness and followed him in rebellion against God.* According to the book of Revelation, a third of the angels in heaven were bewitched by Lucifer and cast down to the earth (see Revelation 12:4, Revelation 12:9).

The Bible calls these demonic angels "stars." The Hollywood Walk of Fame—with its "stars on the ground"—is *a spiritual shrine to the "grounded stars of Satan."* It's no surprise that you will find Satan's shrine in the "City of the Angels"—Los Angeles—also known as the "City of *Lost* Angels." The lost angel-stars followed Lucifer—the bright shining star. These angelic "stars" of Hollywood influence the *entire world* through movies, music, and social media. They are *still participating in a rebellion of sin* against God. Female flesh worship, money worship, and obsession with fame are among the major tricks of their trade. They cause the men, women, boys, and girls of this world to trade their souls for the things of men.

> *But He turned and said to Peter, "Get behind Me, Satan! You are an offense to Me, for you are not mindful of the things of God, but the things of men."* (Matthew 16:23)

The woman of Revelation 12:5 who gives birth to the Man-Child who will defeat all nations is *Israel*. The Man-Child, of course, is Jesus (Revelation 19:15). The Dragon of Revelation 12 tries to destroy the woman (Israel), the Man-Child (Jesus), and the remainder of the woman's children:

> *And the dragon was enraged with the woman, and he went to make war with the rest of her offspring, who keep the commandments of God and have the testimony of Jesus Christ.* (Revelation 12:17)

Lucifer, the beautiful Dragon, is still trying to destroy Israel. He believes if he can kill the people the Lord uses to deliver His Word to mankind, he can stop the prophecies of God. Lustrous Lucifer is the reason why Iran and many other Muslim countries want to wipe Israel off the map. The Muslims and the Jews are spiritual half-brothers through Abraham—their common ancestor. But just like Lucifer inspired Cain to kill his brother Able, he also wants the Muslims to kill the Jews.

Lucifer possessed Pharaoh, king of Egypt. He possessed King Herod when he tried to kill the child Jesus. He possessed Judas Iscariot (see John 6:70, John 13:27). He also possessed Adolph Hitler, the German dictator. Lucifer, the drop dead beautiful, gorgeous angel inspired Hitler and the Germans to kill six million Jews. They also killed many others who didn't fit their model of white aryan supremacy. Lucifer, inside the heart and mind of Hitler, became the gorgeous angel who started a race war.

Only let your conduct be worthy of the gospel of Christ, so that whether I come and see you or am absent, I may hear of your affairs, that you stand fast in one spirit, with one mind striving together for the faith of the gospel. . . . Fulfill my joy by being like-minded, having the same love, being of one accord, of one mind.
Philippians 1:27; 2:2

CHAPTER 6

❋

God Is Not the Creator of Divisiveness

"If a kingdom is divided against itself, that kingdom cannot stand. And if a house is divided against itself, that house cannot stand." Mark 3:24–25

IT WAS JESUS WHO said that a divided house cannot stand, meaning that the Church He is building for the kingdom of God will *not* be divided (see Matthew 16:18). If church members are fostering divisions based on race, economic status, or political affiliation, one of two things are true about that church: 1) Jesus is not the Leader of that church, or 2) that church is in a spiritually immature and infantile state:

> *And I, brethren, could not speak to you as to spiritual people but as to carnal, as to babes in Christ. I fed you with milk and not with solid food; for until now you were not able to receive it, and even now you are still not able; for you are still*

carnal. For where there are envy, strife, and di-
visions among you, are you not carnal and be-
having like mere men? (1 Corinthians 3:1–3)

In the early years of the Church, believers were in one accord (see Acts 2:1–4). The unity in the Spirit that the first church had produced joy, fellowship, friendship, and miracles of faith:

All the believers devoted themselves to the apostles'
teaching, and to fellowship, and to sharing in meals
(including the Lord's Supper), and to prayer. A deep
sense of awe came over them all, and the apostles
performed many miraculous signs and wonders.
And all the believers met together in one place and
shared everything they had. (Acts 2:42–44 NLT)

The Lord didn't only use the apostles to perform miracles. God also used some of the church deacons to perform heavenly signs (see Acts 6:8; 8:5–7). God sent Philip—the miracle working deacon—to introduce the Gospel of Jesus to an Ethiopian Jew:

Now an angel of the Lord spoke to Philip, saying,
"Arise and go toward the south along the road which
goes down from Jerusalem to Gaza." This is desert.
So he arose and went. And behold, a man of Ethiopia,
a eunuch of great authority under Candace the
queen of the Ethiopians, who had charge of all her
treasury, and had come to Jerusalem to worship, was
returning. And sitting in his chariot, he was read-
ing Isaiah the prophet. Then the Spirit said to Philip,
"Go near and overtake this chariot." So Philip ran to
him, and heard him reading the prophet Isaiah, and
said, "Do you understand what you are reading?"
And he said, "How can I, unless someone guides

me?" And he asked Philip to come up and sit with him. The place in the Scripture which he read was this: "He was led as a sheep to the slaughter; and as a lamb before its shearer is silent, So He opened not His mouth. In His humiliation His justice was taken away, and who will declare His generation? For His life is taken from the earth." So the eunuch answered Philip and said, "I ask you, of whom does the prophet say this, of himself or of some other man?" Then Philip opened his mouth, and beginning at this Scripture, preached Jesus to him. Now as they went down the road, they came to some water. And the eunuch said, "See, here is water. What hinders me from being baptized?" Then Philip said, "If you believe with all your heart, you may." And he answered and said, "I believe that Jesus Christ is the Son of God." So he commanded the chariot to stand still. And both Philip and the eunuch went down into the water, and he baptized him. (Acts 8:26–38)

That Ethiopian probably had skin as black as charcoal. Yet God cared about him. He cared so much that he sent Philip into the desert to meet him and teach him about Jesus. I'm sorry to have to say this, but that black man would not be welcome in a certain white church that I've visited. If he were—for political correctness—accepted into that church, he would remain a second-class citizen. I also attended another church that had the same attitude toward Christians who don't look like they are related to Barbie and Ken.

Jesus prayed for a oneness in His Church that could be seen by the world:

"I pray that they will all be one, just as you and I are one—as you are in me, Father, and I am in you. And

may they be in us so that the world will believe you sent me. I have given them the glory you gave me, so they may be one as we are one. I am in them and you are in me. May they experience such perfect unity that the world will know that you sent me and that you love them as much as you love me." (John 17:21–23 NLT)

A worldwide unified Church is what Jesus prayed for. Yet many churches in the world are anything but united. They are mostly divided by race, politics, economic status, and denominational creeds. Why? And what is the remedy for such divisiveness?

A big part of the problem is a lack of spiritual maturity in the pulpits—and consequently in the pews. It is *rare* to find a preacher who preaches more than the basics of Hebrews 6:1–2:

So let us stop going over the basic teachings about Christ again and again. Let us go on instead and become mature in our understanding. Surely we don't need to start again with the fundamental importance of repenting from evil deeds and placing our faith in God. You don't need further instruction about baptisms, the laying on of hands, the resurrection of the dead, and eternal judgment. (NLT)

Sunday after Sunday, week after week, month after month, and year after year, many church members are fed a watered-down version of Hebrews 6:1–2. Their spiritual growth is retarded from a biblical diet that's lacking in diversity. They get stuck in the *infantile loop* that Hebrews 5:12–13 explains:

For though by this time you ought to be teachers, you need someone to teach you again the first principles of the oracles of God; and you

have come to need milk and not solid food. For
everyone who partakes only of milk is unskilled
in the word of righteousness, for he is a babe.

Hebrews 6:1 (KJV) exhorts Christians to do this:

"Leaving the principles of the doctrine of Christ
let us go on to <u>perfection</u>" (emphasis added).

This phrase contains the key to the infantile loop problem that is so common in churches. "Perfection" in this verse, of course, means "completion." Jesus used the word *perfect* to mean something similar:

"But I say to you, love your enemies, bless those who
curse you, do good to those who hate you, and pray
for those who spitefully use you and persecute you,
that you may be sons of your Father in heaven; for
He makes His sun rise on the evil and on the good,
and sends rain on the just and on the unjust. For
if you love those who love you, what reward have
you? Do not even the tax collectors do the same?
And if you greet your brethren only, what do you
do more than others? Do not even the tax collectors
do so? Therefore you shall be perfect, just as your
Father in heaven is perfect." (Matthew 5:44–48)

The perfection that Jesus wants you to achieve is *unconditional love.* Love your enemies, love your friends, love your neighbors, love your country, pray for your President, pray for your political leaders, and *love all races that God created.* God *is* love:

Beloved, let us love one another: for love is of
God; and every one that loveth is born of God,

and knoweth God. He that loveth not knoweth not God; for God is love. (1 John 4:7–8 KJV)

It is God's love that will make your mind a holy place:

Love suffers long and is kind; love does not envy; love does not parade itself, is not puffed up; does not behave rudely, does not seek its own, is not provoked, thinks no evil. (1 Corinthians 13:4–5)

God's love in your mind will make it a place where God is welcomed. God's love in your mind will make it a place where God wants to stay. God's love in your mind will make it complete. God's love in your mind will make it perfect.

But when that which is perfect has come, then that which is in part will be done away. (1 Corinthians 13:10)

God's love is the most powerful medicine in the world. It neutralizes dissention, disputes, and disagreements between people. Differences between believers become unimportant in its presence. It is more important than money, wisdom, faith, knowledge, and acts of charity. Love is the Greatest Commandment (see Matthew 22:36–40). God's love is the antivenom for the Serpent poison of animosity and hatred. It is *the cure* for division in a church.

God's love in your mind will erase all traces of hate from your thoughts. God's love will make your mind a heavenly place. And you will know there is no race in the heavenly place.

*"The people have appointed kings without my consent,
and princes without my knowledge."*
Hosea 8:4 NLT

CHAPTER 7

Voting Is Not the Eleventh Commandment

Then all the elders of Israel gathered together and came to Samuel [the prophet of God] *at Ramah, and said to him, "Look, you are old, and your sons do not walk in your ways. Now make us a king to judge us like all the nations." But the thing displeased Samuel when they said, "Give us a king to judge us." So Samuel prayed to the LORD. And the LORD said to Samuel, "Heed the voice of the people in all that they say to you; for they have not rejected you, but they have rejected Me, that I should not reign over them. According to all the works which they have done since the day that I brought them up out of Egypt, even to this day—with which they have forsaken Me and served other gods—so they are doing to you also.*

Now therefore, heed their voice. However, you shall
solemnly forewarn them, and show them the behavior
of the king who will reign over them." 1 Samuel 8:4–9

WHEN THE ELDERS OF Israel decided to trade their holy leader for a political boss man, God said that the change in leadership was idolatry. After all, God's vision for Israel when they left Egypt's slavery was a priesthood nation:

> *Then Moses climbed the mountain to appear before*
> *God. The LORD called to him from the mountain and*
> *said, "Give these instructions . . . to the descendants*
> *of Israel: 'You have seen what I did to the Egyptians*
> *. . . Now if you will obey me and keep my covenant,*
> *you will be my own special treasure from among all*
> *the peoples on earth . . . And you will be my king-*
> *dom of priests, my holy nation.' This is the message*
> *you must give to the people of Israel." So Moses re-*
> *turned from the mountain and called together the*
> *elders of the people and told them everything the*
> *LORD had commanded him. And all the people re-*
> *sponded together, "We will do everything the LORD*
> *has commanded." So Moses brought the people's*
> *answer back to the LORD.* (Exodus 19:3–8 NLT)

The elders of Israel during this time decided Samuel should be succeeded by a secular king rather than his dishonest sons. They didn't have the faith and the patience to wait for the Lord to give them a God-fearing leader. They wanted to be like the rest of the world and be led by a political ruler.

Samuel eventually appointed Saul as the first king of Israel (see 1 Samuel 10:1–11). King Saul was successful at first, but his tragic mistake was trying to fill Samuel's shoes as a prophet of the Lord:

Saul waited there seven days for Samuel, as Samuel had instructed him earlier, but Samuel still didn't come. Saul realized that his troops were rapidly slipping away. So he demanded, "Bring me the burnt offering and the peace offerings!" And Saul sacrificed the burnt offering himself. Just as Saul was finishing with the burnt offering, Samuel arrived. Saul went out to meet and welcome him, but Samuel said, "What is this you have done?" Saul replied, "I saw my men scattering from me, and you didn't arrive when you said you would, and the Philistines are at Micmash ready for battle. So I said, 'The Philistines are ready to march against us at Gilgal, and I haven't even asked for the LORD's help!' So I felt compelled to offer the burnt offering myself before you came." "How foolish!" Samuel exclaimed. "You have not kept the command the LORD your God gave you. Had you kept it, the LORD would have established your kingdom over Israel forever. But now your kingdom must end, for the LORD has sought out a man after his own heart. The LORD has already appointed him to be the leader of his people, because you have not kept the LORD's command." (1 Samuel 13:8–14 NLT)

From that time, Saul began a slow decline into obsessive jealousy, murderous anger, fear, and bouts of insanity (see 1 Samuel 18:7–12; 20:27–34). He eventually killed himself during a battle with the Philistines:

The fighting grew very fierce around Saul, and the Philistine archers caught up with him and wounded him severely. Saul groaned to his armor bearer, "Take your sword and kill me before these pagan Philistines come to run me through and

taunt and torture me." But his armor bearer was
afraid and would not do it. So Saul took his own
sword and fell on it. When his armor bearer real-
ized that Saul was dead, he fell on his own sword
and died beside the king. (1 Samuel 31:3–5 NLT)

God instructed Samuel to choose David as the next king of
Israel (see 1 Samuel 16:1–13). David was a spiritual-minded
man who became Israel's singing prophet (see 2 Samuel 23:1–
2). King David wrote many of the psalms (songs) in the Bible.
He was the only King of Israel whom God allowed to wear the
clothes of a priest:

> *David danced before the* LORD *with all his might,*
> *wearing a priestly garment.* (2 Samuel 6:14 NLT)

David—the prophet, priest, and king—came closer than
anyone else to fulfilling God's vision of an Israeli "kingdom of
priests." He was a *prophetic prototype* of the Messiah of God. The
"Star of David" on Israel's national flag is a symbol of the Messiah—a descendant of David.

> *The* LORD *swore an oath to David with a promise*
> *he will never take back: "I will place one of your de-*
> *scendants on your throne . . . then your royal line will*
> *continue forever and ever."* (Psalm 132:11–12 NLT)

Christians know that Jesus Christ was born on earth through
Mary—a descendant of David. We know that Jesus—the one
they called the Son of David—is the Messiah who has come and
will come again:

> *Jesus was in the center of the procession, and the*
> *people all around him were shouting, "Praise*

God for the Son of David! Blessings on the one who comes in the name of the LORD! Praise God in highest heaven!" (Matthew 21:9 NLT)

Unlike Saul, King David and King Jesus were not chosen by the will of people. David and Jesus were chosen by the will of God.

The government that was led by King Saul did everything in its power to kill David. But the Lord protected him, and he eventually became God's appointed king of Israel.

Likewise, the government during Jesus's earthly ministry did everything in its power to destroy Him. King Herod tried to kill Him but failed. Pontius Pilate tried to release Jesus from arrest, but he was persuaded to execute Him by the religious authorities. They made him afraid of offending Caesar, the Roman emperor:

Pilate went outside again and said to the people, "I am going to bring him out to you now, but understand clearly that I find him not guilty." Then Jesus came out wearing the crown of thorns and the purple robe. And Pilate said, "Look, here is the man!" When they saw him, the leading priests and Temple guards began shouting, "Crucify him! Crucify him!" "Take him yourselves and crucify him," Pilate said. "I find him not guilty.". . . Then Pilate tried to release him, but the Jewish leaders shouted, "If you release this man, you are no 'friend of Caesar.' Anyone who declares himself a king is a rebel against Caesar." When they said this, Pilate brought Jesus out to them again . . . . And Pilate said to the people, "Look, here is your king!" "Away with him," they yelled. "Away with him! Crucify him!" "What? Crucify your king?" Pilate asked. "We have no king but Caesar," the leading

*priests shouted back. Then Pilate turned Jesus over
to them to be crucified.* (John 19:4–6, 12–17 NLT)

The high priest and his cohorts committed blatant idolatry
when they rejected Jesus—the Word of God—for the dictates
of Caesar's government. Pilate knew Jesus was innocent. He
knew the priests were motivated by jealousy. And he knew they
were manipulating the Roman system of government to get rid
of Him. He knew the truth of the situation. But in spite of his
knowledge, Pilate had to adhere to a system of government that
says the voice of the majority must prevail. The Roman system
of government had to be revered and upheld—even if it meant
trampling the truth on the ground.

Let me be clear about this: The union of government and religion crucified Jesus. It was the vote of the majority of the leading
priests that caused an innocent Man to be executed—and a guilty
man to be released:

> *But they were insistent, demanding with loud voices
> that He be crucified. And the voices of these men and
> of the chief priests prevailed. So Pilate gave sentence
> that it should be as they requested. And he released
> to them the one they requested* [Barabbas], *who for
> rebellion and murder had been thrown into prison;
> but he delivered Jesus to their will.* (Luke 23:23–25)

When the Catholic Church gained governmental authority in
the Dark Ages, they killed thousands of Christians. They continued their campaign of murder using government and religious
authority during the Protestant Reformation. They persecuted
and killed the Anabaptists (the forerunners of modern Mennonite and Amish churches). The Amish and the Mennonites have
not forgotten that the government was the enemy of their faith.
They came to America so that they could be free to worship

God without governmental control. To this day, most Amish and Mennonite church members do not vote for government political leaders.

According to current Evangelical Christian teaching, the Amish and the Mennonites who refuse to vote are not doing their God-given duty. Evangelicals have made voting the "Eleventh Commandment." They try to hang heavy drapes of guilt on anyone who doesn't vote.

It is *my duty* to say that voting is *not* the Eleventh Commandment. God is not going to cast anyone into hell because he or she didn't vote. This Eleventh Commandment to vote is a teaching from men—not from God. It is a clear example of Mark 7:7 (NLT): "Their worship is a farce, for they teach man-made ideas as commands from God."

I know some very godly Mennonite Christians. They have never voted and never will vote. Nevertheless, their lives embody these verses:

> *Make it your goal to live a quiet life, minding your own business and working with your hands, just as we instructed you before. Then people who are not Christians will respect the way you live, and you will not need to depend on others.* (1 Thessalonians 4:11–12 NLT)

The Mennonites support the government by being exemplary citizens. I suspect they obey 1 Timothy 2:1–3 (NLT):

> *I urge you, first of all, to pray for all people. Ask God to help them; intercede on their behalf, and give thanks for them. Pray this way for kings and all who are in authority so that we can live peaceful and quiet lives marked by godliness and dignity. This is good and pleases God our Savior.*

The Mennonites that I know are God-fearing people. They have reverence for God, and they respect the government. Their lives obey Jesus's command to give Caesar the things that belong to Caesar, and give God the things that belong to God (see Mark 12:17). My Mennonite friends are the salt of the earth. They know that voting is not the Eleventh Commandment.

One of the founding principles of our government is freedom of religion. Everyone in our country knows that he or she is free to choose a religion—or no religion. The government does not compel anyone to worship in a particular manner.

By now you probably think I am trying to persuade people not to vote for government leaders. That is not the case. I think everyone should be *free* to vote or not vote according to the dictates of his or her conscience. No one should feel *pressured* to participate in any electoral process. I believe Romans 14:22 (NLT) should be one's guide when it comes to voting or not voting:

> *You may believe there's nothing wrong with what you are doing, but keep it between yourself and God. Blessed are those who don't feel guilty for doing something they have decided is right.*

I recently read an article about a man and his wife who were driving to their Baptist church to vote in a US Senate election. The man collapsed on the way to the church precinct. He was taken to the hospital, where he died. Election officials had high praise for the wife—because she went back later to cast her ballot. That wife's choice to go vote—within hours of her husband's death—*is between her and God.* It is likely that she was taught—and believed—that voting is God's will. Many churches teach that voting for government officials is the will of God. For them, support for the government by voting is the Eleventh Commandment.

Our government exercises considerable control over the majority of churches in our country. Most churches want the tax-exempt status that the government offers. In order for a church to qualify for tax exemption, it must be managed like a corporate business. It must be led by a board of directors that is appointed by a vote of the members of the church. Church officers, including the lead pastor, are appointed by an *electoral process*. The church must maintain corporate bylaws that specify how often board members or other officers are selected. The church must maintain records of all internal elections, finances, and other business processes. All church records must be readily available for an IRS audit at any time.

This governmental control causes many churches to become good businesses—but at the expense of fostering the comforting presence of God. These churches are *not* sanctuaries of solace from the stresses of the world. Rather, they are *extensions of the world—with Jesus's name attached*. That is why many churches are infected with infighting, power struggles, strife, and division. Some churches are cold, dark places of death instead of places where hearts are filled with Light and the warm welcome of God.

Take a look at what Jesus Himself said to the last church that He personally spoke to:

> *"I know your works, that you are neither cold nor hot. I could wish you were cold or hot. So then, because you are lukewarm, and neither cold nor hot, I will vomit you out of My mouth. Because you say, 'I am rich, have become wealthy, and have need of nothing'—and do not know that you are wretched, miserable, poor, blind, and naked."* (Revelation 3:15–17)

This is what happens when a church is governed by the laws of men instead of leadership by the Holy Spirit of God.

67

The pastor who has a true calling from the Lord will recuse himself from most of the business and the busy-ness of running a church. Like the apostles in Acts 6:2–4, he will delegate the secular functions of church work and devote himself to prayer, preaching and teaching, and tending to the needs of the flock of God.

There is coming a time when all the nations of earth will be ruled by righteous leaders appointed by God:

> *Look, a righteous king is coming! And honest princes will rule under him.* (Isaiah 32:1 NLT)

History is His story. It is the story of the fall of the first Adam in the beginning—and the rise of the Last Adam at the end.

> *The Scriptures tell us, "The first man, Adam, became a living person." But the last Adam—that is, Christ— is a life-giving Spirit.* (1 Corinthians 15:45 NLT)

One day, Jesus Christ will return to earth and set up His government. Then the prophecies of Isaiah will be fulfilled:

> *For unto us a Child is born, unto us a Son is given; and the government will be upon His shoulder. And His name will be called Wonderful, Counselor, Mighty God, Everlasting Father, Prince of Peace. Of the increase of His government and peace there will be no end, upon the throne of David and over His kingdom, to order it and establish it with judgment and justice from that time forward, even forever. The zeal of the LORD of hosts will perform this.* (Isaiah 9:6–7)

True Christians are eagerly waiting for the day that they meet Jesus face-to-face. We are eagerly waiting for the time that Jesus sets up the kingdom of God on earth. We are more than ready for God's new heaven and new earth. We have not lost sight of the Word of God. We believe the promises of God.

Nevertheless we, according to His promise, look for new heavens and a new earth in which righteousness dwells. Therefore, beloved, looking forward to these things, be diligent to be found by Him in peace, without spot and blameless.
(2 Peter 3:13–14)

www.ingramcontent.com/pod-product-compliance
Lightning Source LLC
Chambersburg PA
CBHW060653030426
42337CB00017B/2586